the joy of affection

Augusto D. Mello

illustrations by Trevor Murphy

DEAR RATNADEVA

MAY THE DHARMA, THE BUDHA & THE SANGHA KEEP POWERFULLY TAKING YOU TO THE OTHER SHORE :)

♥ of AUGUSTO

For Giulia
my eternal rainbow

The one you are looking for

Everyone one meets,

is the one

one needs to meet.

A lesson, a good challenge, a love story,

a potential healer, someone to heal.

A priceless friend,

one to receive a gift from,

or to bestow a gift.

A guide or one to be guided.

Everyone one meets,

is the one

one needs to meet.

Breathe deeply.

Be present.

The one you are looking for

at the unique moment we call now,

is always

right next to you.

Interdependence

We are masters of cooperation,

beings of affection from the moment we are born;

who thrive, once warmly held and cared for,

yet who struggle so much when affection is not present.

Affection creates strong emotional bonds

and a natural drive to cooperate.

Together

we laugh, cry, support and challenge one another.

And together we create!

We embrace our soft feet with shoes

and explore the wildest terrains of the world;

we fly with borrowed metallic wings

making possible the apparently impossible.

Sharing affection in a safe environment is delicious.

It's delicious because it's our nature.

Look attentively with an open mind

and you might be surprised to find

how common gentle affection is amongst us.

Without affection we would not survive,

let alone thrive

in this big, blue, beautiful ball,

we call Earth.

How valuable affection is

The value of affection

is the value of a gentle nod, a smile,

a caring and a loving word,

the value of a good laugh,

a gentle touch of hands,

the value there is in forgiving others,

and above all ourselves.

The value of *allowing* affection

to flourish in our hearts;

affection for all there is and all there isn't,

for all we are and all we are not.

It's the value of a big long cuddle

of a 5 year old child

as they cover us gently

with their favourite

blankey.

What affection is, how affection feels

Affection is better than chocolate.

Better than chocolate I assure you, it is.

Affection is a *practice*.

A *practice* that is easy, natural and sweet,

like a ripe mango from a tree

on the most beautiful afternoon

that may be.

How to practice affection

We are affection,

we just forgot that we are.

The heart of a new born baby

is the heart we were all born with.

Practicing affection is just

gently *allowing* ourselves to reconnect

with that soft heart,

whilst the mind matures

and our natural affectionate instincts

guide our actions.

Music

We are a fine tuned orchestra

of wondrous beauty,

capable of

playing a Cosmic Song

of pure happiness,

warmed up by

a*llowing* affection in,

and played out beautifully

by *allowing* affection to flow out

unconditionally.

Love, Affection's partner

If love were a light bulb

which can be bright, bringing fun and joy

to the darkest night;

affection would be electricity,

empowering, making sure it comes to life.

When together and together expressed,

they become pure bliss,

harmony and light.

However, at times, we expect one another

to fulfil our fantasies of what each other 'should be';

rather than celebrating and being surprised

by who we actually are.

Through our expectations, we can only see ourselves

and what we want.

An unconscious prison of mirrors.

In isolation, affection is not *allowed* in, or *practiced.*

Inevitably, the result is darkness and pain.

People who profoundly love one another,

profoundly hurt one another;

just because they haven't realised

that love without its partner, affection,

becomes bitter with loneliness.

Big cats

At times when we feel

threatened, hurt or challenged,

affection shrinks within our hearts

and anger settles in.

We learnt in ancient times

that anger works well

to make us stronger for fighting;

it saved us in the past

from hungry big cats

with hungry big mouths

and hungry big teeth.

Now the big cats are in big natural reserves.

But we still get angry

if we feel threatened, hurt or challenged,

sometimes by the ones we love most.

Then many of us end up

acting as if we were facing

hungry big cats

in ancient times.

Dealing with anger

Humility

calms the mind, body and spirit.

When our heart gets hurt,

we feel threatened or challenged,

and anger comes, as it naturally does,

and it's okay to feel angry;

the angrier we get

the humbler we shall act,

the softer we ought to speak,

firm if necessary, but always kind.

Naturally, we will eventually realise

anger is just a cover up for emotional pain.

And it's okay to feel emotional pain.

We then might feel sadness,

And it's okay to be sad,

maybe we will experience fear,

And it's okay to be scared.

By embracing the reality of emotional pain

without struggle, defenceless,

the delusions brought up by anger start to dispel

and we start to gain real strength.

Rather than hardening, our heart softens

and the real healing process

finally begins.

It's okay to be you

It's okay.

It's really okay.

It's okay to be okay or not.

And as much as it's okay to enjoy being okay,

it is equally okay to be angry for not being okay.

Its really okay

to be you,

in all that you are,

in all you are not,

right here,

right now.

A powerful gift

Gently and kindly

empowering every breath you take

with affection towards yourself and others,

is one of the most

healing, powerful and wonderful

practices and gifts

you can give to yourself,

others and life itself.

Rainbow

If we turn our attention

defencelessly inwards

we might notice

that our inner and outer lives

radiate colours abundantly,

as a rainbow of infinite hues;

and what others can see

is just a glimpse

of who we are.

However, a tiny flash of pure light

is nonetheless as pure

as the light of a billion stars,

as pure as light always is.

Practising affection is

to embrace

and cherish

each other

by noticing and celebrating

the infinitely exquisite

multicoloured light

we all share.

You are WOWSOME!

Whoever you are,

wherever you are,

whatever happened,

however you feel,

whatever your thoughts,

dreams and fantasies,

you are WOWSOME !

Practicing affection is celebrating

each other's WOWSOMENESS!

Never be afraid to learn from the masters

We live amongst masters of affection.

The ones that with a mere glimpse,

or the slightest touch

can instantly feed the "most starved of hearts"

with the pure nectar of affection.

They are unassuming and of pure humility.

One night, one of them skilfully taught me

what the ultimate *practice of affection* is.

It is simply, unconditionally *allowing* affection to guide us;

no agendas, no expectations, no judgments;

of the king or the pauper

without distinction.

The master I met that night

rather than expecting me to kneel or bow,

showered me with pure, genuine affection.

Not concerned by who I was or was not.

I think he was homeless;

but that didn't matter to him,

It mattered perhaps only to the human

seated on the street with his dog,

smiling as he held the master's leash.

How to be affectionate to a cactus

Some people have had their hearts pricked.

And to avoid any more prickles

they protect their heart, with guess what?

Even more prickles; and that really hurts, themselves above all.

I affectionately call them cactus guys and gals.

I was once a cactus guy.

However, the more I practice affection

the more naturally affectionate I get.

And believe you me, as one gets more affectionate,

The cuddlier one gets as well

and the prickles start to fall as the heart gets softer.

It's just natural.

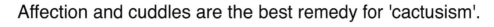

Affection and cuddles are the best remedy for 'cactusism'.

But how can a cactus be cuddled?

Cuddles can be done

not only with arms,

but with gentle hands and fingers between the prickles;

or cuddly words or cuddly actions or gestures.

Have you ever looked at someone

and felt cuddled by their eyes?

You see, we can cuddle with anything!

From head to toe.

I just love toe cuddling!

Affection in action

I was in a queue when a big angry guy

bounced in front of me with a hard push.

Naturally, anger set in within me too

How contagious it is!

But I decided to *practice* affection

and *allowed* myself to feel affection for him

even though he emotionally hurt me.

It felt different but not too difficult, really!

It actually was easy once I made the choice;

as anger and affection cannot coexist.

As I *allowed* affection to set in

the tension and anger gently melted away.

I looked at him affectionately, he looked really tired.

Following my instincts I gently said:

"It seems you had a hard day man",

not trying 'to fix' him although it softened his emotions.

I just wanted to connect with someone I felt affection for.

He turned around and talked, and talked..

He was emotionally hurt, overworked and burned out.

I suggested he take respite with the ones he loved most

and loved him back just the same.

We shook hands and he left peacefully.

Such a special moment which could have been so different.

It was incredibly healing for us both.

How do I know how far I can go?

The more I live in affection

the happier I get

and the happier I naturally make others,

without trying to make them happy.

The more I live in affection

the air feels fresher as it cuddles me,

the water tastes delicious as it cuddles my tongue and I

cuddle them back.

The more I see and feel the WOWSOMENESS

of this experience we call life,

as I naturally cuddle it

with all I am and am not

and feel life embracing and cuddling me back.

The more affectionate I become,

the more I see and connect

with my real essence

which resembles more and more

that long forgotten essence

of a newborn baby.

Pure Peace, pure Love, pure Joy.

Although the words

Love, and Peace and Joy

cannot describe

that feeling which

transcends concepts.

What next?

Affection is an ongoing *practice;*

a practice of *allowing* affection to take over;

followed by trusting our instincts.

As I practice affection regularly

it starts to become second nature.

As I practice more,

naturally it will grow simply into nature.

We can choose now to be affectionate beings

just by a*llowing* affection to spurt like a fountain

of pure nectar,

always delicious, caring and fresh,

coloured by the infinite rainbow hues that we are.

Together we can gently heal one another
and end emotional starvation.
And finally, feeling
safe, accepted and celebrated,
we might realise ourselves
as manifestations of love unbounded,
enjoying every day more of the purest
Joy of Affection.

May your life be full of

happiness, joy, peace of

mind, laughter and many,

many warm cuddles!

Augusto and Trev

:)

Printed in Great Britain
by Amazon

21072375R00025